MAY 2 4 2016

W9-BCM-139

CHILDREN LIKE US

Homes

AROUND THE WORLD

Moira Butterfield

Cavendish
Square
New York

Published in 2016 by Cavendish Square Publishing, LLC
243 5th Avenue, Suite 136, New York, NY 10016

Website: cavendishsq.com

This publication represents the opinions and views of the author based on his or her personal experience, knowledge, and research. The information in this book serves as a general guide only. The author and publisher have used their best efforts in preparing this book and disclaim liability rising directly or indirectly from the use and application of this book.

CPSIA Compliance Information: Batch #WW16CSQ

All websites were available and accurate when this book was sent to press.However, it is possible that contents or addresses may have changed since the publication of this book. No responsibility for any such changes can be accepted by either the author or the Publisher.

Cataloging-in-Publication Data

Butterfield, Moira.
Homes around the world / by Moira Butterfield.
p. cm. — (Children like us)
Includes index.
ISBN 978-1-5026-0844-4 (hardcover) ISBN 978-1-5026-0842-0 (paperback) ISBN 978-1-5026-0845-1 (ebook)
1. Dwellings — Juvenile literature. 2. Dwellings — Cross-cultural studies — Juvenile literature.
3. Housing — Juvenile literature. I. Butterfield, Moira, 1960-. II. Title.
GT172.B88 2016
643'.1—d23

Editor: Izzi Howell
Designer: Kevin Knight
Proofreaders: Izzi Howell/Stephen White-Thomson
Picture researcher: Izzi Howell
Wayland editor: Annabel Stones

Picture credits:
The author and publisher would like to thank the following for allowing their pictures to be reproduced in this publication: cover np/Shutterstock.com; p.3 (t-b) powerofforever/iStock, bpperry/iStock, Kingarion/Shutterstock, Victoria Lipov/Shutterstock; pp.4-5 (c) ekler/Shutterstock; p.4 (t) Victoria Lipov/Shutterstock, (b) Edyta Pawlowska/Shutterstock; p.5 (tl) gkuna/Shutterstock, (tr) Attila Jandi/Shutterstock, (b) andyKrakovski/iStock; p.6 (tr) Edyta Pawlowska/Shutterstock, (bl) f9photos/Shutterstock, (br) bpperry/Shutterstock; p.7 Ijam Hairi/Shutterstock; p.8 (tl) Yavuz Sariyildiz/Shuttestock, (br) Andrew Rich/iStock; p.9 (l) Sophie James/Shutterstock, (r) Victoria Lipov/Shutterstock; p.10 (t) Skafrica/iStock, (b) Alison Wright/Corbis; p.11 (t) Nicolas Marino/NA/Novarc/Corbis, (b) withGod/Shutterstock; p.12 (tr) Joe Gough/Shutterstock, (bl) andyKrakovski/iStock, (br) Kashper/Shutterstock; p.13 Jane Sweeney/Robert Harding World Imagery/Corbis; p.14 (t) Anne-Christine Poujoulat/Getty Images, (b) Rikke Skaaning/Keystone/Corbis; p.15 YinYang/iStock; p.16 (tl) Attila Jandi/Shutterstock, (cr) Nico Tondini/Robert Harding World Imagery/Corbis, (br) A.S. Zain/Shutterstock; p.17 Michael Freeman/Corbis; p.18 (tr) powerofforever/iStock, (cr) nevereverro/iStock, (bl) Ryusuke Komori/Shutterstock; p.19 Jerome Levitch/Corbis; p.20 (tl) Dutourdumonde Photography/Shutterstock, (tr) Zzvet/Shutterstock, (br) gkuna/iStock; p.21 Eric Lafforgue/arabianEye/Corbis; p.22 (tl) Christian Wheatley/iStock, (cr) Padmayogini/Shutterstock, (bl) Nathan Alliard/ /Photononstop/Corbis; p.23 vitalez/Shutterstock; p.24 (tr) Mike Feeney/Eye Ubiquitous/Corbis, (bl) somor/iStock, (br) Natalia Sidorova/Shutterstock; p.25 (t) vkph/iStock, (b) Philippe Giraud/Sygma/Corbis; p.26 (t) Nikada/iStock, (b) Hector Conesa/Shutterstock; p.27 Lindsay Hebberd/Corbis; p.28 (t) Kingarion/Shutterstock, (b) Maxim Lysenko/Shutterstock; p.29 Marafona/Shutterstock; p.30 (l-r, t-b) vitalez/Shutterstock, Nikada/iStock, Andrew Rich/iStock, Ryusuke Komori/Shutterstock, somor/iStock, Attila Jandi/Shutterstock, withGod/Shutterstock, Kashper/Shutterstock, Kingarion/Shutterstock, gkuna/iStock, Joe Gough/Shutterstock, f9photos/Shutterstock, Victoria Lipov/Shutterstock, Maxim Lysenko/Shutterstock; p.31 (l) A.S. Zain/Shutterstock, Marafona/Shutterstock.

Design elements used throughout: vectorkat/Shutterstock, lilac/Shutterstock, rassco/Shutterstock, tereez/Shutterstock, Val_Iva/Shutterstock, Dacian G/Shutterstock, DVARG/Shutterstock, Spreadthesign/Shutterstock, Oceloti/Shutterstock, kanarina/Shutterstock, lalan/Shutterstock, katarina_1/Shutterstock, tereez/Shutterstock, Marchie/Shutterstock, Masha Tace/Shutterstock, Sushko Anastasia/Shutterstock, ecco/Shutterstock, notkoo/Shutterstock, jehsomwang/Shutterstock.

Printed in the United States of America

Contents

All Kinds of Homes

Children around the world live in homes just as you do. However, not all these homes are the same. You'll learn about houseboats that float on water. You'll learn about desert tents that can be moved around, too.

City homes are packed together in tall buildings. Learn more about these apartments on page 9.

Some homes are built on water. Turn to page 6 to find out about the homes of the Peruvian Uros people.

Some people live high in the mountains. Learn why many Italian villages are built high up on page 20.

Can you guess how many families live together in this longhouse in Borneo? Find out the answer on page 16.

Find out about the painted homes of the Tiebele people in Burkina Faso on page 26.

Take a trip around the world to discover the homes of children just like you!

Homes on the Water

The homes in this Andean village are made of reeds. So is the island they sit on.

The Uros people live in South America. They live in the Andes Mountains on Lake Titicaca. For centuries, the Uros people have been living on floating islands. They are made out of reeds that grow in the lake.

Kerala in India is famous for its houseboats. In Vancouver, Canada, there is a whole village of houses built on floating platforms in the sea.

This Indian barge may once have carried rice or spices. Today, it is a houseboat.

These are the floating homes off the coast of Vancouver, Canada. You might row over to your neighbor's house!

The Bajau people of Malaysia live in houses on the sea. Their homes are made from wood and dried plants. They stand on long wooden poles pushed into the sea floor.

These Bajau children row to and from their house.

Homes in the City

1.8 million people live in houses in the shantytowns of Delhi in India.

Many cities around the world have shantytowns. These are places where people live in shacks they have built themselves. They often have no running water or electricity.

This Brazilian boy lives in a favela. This is the name used for shantytowns in South America. Around 11 million Brazilian people live in favelas. Local people are now working to try to improve life in the favelas.

In Brazil, many families use recycled materials to build their homes in the favelas.

Cities are often crowded places, so building up, rather than out, helps to create more homes for everyone. Many city dwellers live in high-rise buildings, in apartments on top of each other.

The world's highest building is Burj Khalifa in Dubai. There are 900 apartments inside the building.

These apartment buildings are in New York. Some of the first high-rise homes were built here.

A Tent Home

The Bedouin people live in North Africa. Some Bedouins are nomads. This means that they move around a lot. They herd animals, such as camels and goats, around the desert. They set up camps wherever they find food and water for their animals.

The inside of a Bedouin tent is kept dark on hot days. This helps it stay cool inside.

This Tibetan girl is making yak butter tea in her tent.

This girl is inside a Tibetan nomad tent. Her family looks after a herd of yaks. They use yak hair to weave the tent fabric. The tent has a stove that burns dried yak dung.

Meat is hung from the walls of the *ger* to dry. Dried meat lasts much longer than fresh meat.

Mongolian people who live on the plains use round tents. They are called *gers*. Living in tents is great for a nomad's life. They pack them up when they need new pasture for their cattle, goats, and horses.

Mongolian families often pitch their *gers* near each other to make small villages.

A Thatched Home

Country homes are sometimes built with things found in the nearby land. This crofter's cottage in Scotland has a thatched roof made from dried reeds. The roof beams of a croft are sometimes made from driftwood found on the beach.

The walls of the Scottish croft are made from stones found nearby.

The Zulu people live in these round, straw-thatched huts. They live in Swaziland in southern Africa. The huts are built in a village called an *umuzi*. They sit inside a fence made of straw.

This Zulu hut has adobe walls. Adobe is mud baked in the sun.

The roofs of these houses in Thailand are made from rain forest grasses.

This tall hut is built by the Dorze people. They live in the Ethiopian mountains. They make their homes from bamboo and the leaves of the "false banana" plant. Each hut is built tall because its base will slowly rot. The huts last about 60 years. Then they become too small to live in.

Inside a Dorze hut, there are benches, beds, and a fireplace There are no windows, though.

A Home on Wheels

The Roma are a group of people who live in many countries across Europe. They often live in caravans. Caravans are large groups of people traveling together in moving homes. They move to places where there is work for them.

This Roma mom and daughter live together in this cozy caravan.

This family belongs to the Yeniche community. The Yeniche are people who like to move often. They live in France, Germany, Switzerland, and Austria.

The Yeniche tend to travel and sell craft goods in summer. They stay in one place in winter.

Taking a trip in a motorhome is like taking your home with you on a trip. A motorhome has a kitchen, bathroom, and bedrooms. It is just like a house, but on wheels!

There aren't many places to stay in Arizona's deserts. A motorhome is like a hotel you bring with you!

Homes Together

A longhouse is a place where lots of families live together. The longhouse here belongs to the Dayak people of Sarawak, Borneo. Around 20–30 families live there. Each family has their own living and sleeping space.

This longhouse is made of bamboo. It is built on stilts so it won't flood in the rainy season.

The longhouse has a corridor that everyone uses to get to their rooms. Animals such as pigs and chickens are kept under the house. Things are stored under the roof.

The private rooms are on the right in this longhouse in Borneo.

In a Dayak longhouse, there is storage room up above, and a place to climb, too!

Chinese *tulous* usually house a group of family members. This is called a clan.

This round building is called a *tulou*. The Hakka people in China live here. Up to 300 people may live in a *tulou*. Each family has its own rooms. However, everyone shares a well. They share supplies, such as wood for their fires, too.

17